★ *GREAT SPORTS TEAMS* ★

## THE DETROIT

## BASKETBALL TEAM

## David Aretha

**Enslow Publishers, Inc.**

| | |
|---|---|
| 40 Industrial Road | PO Box 38 |
| Box 398 | Aldershot |
| Berkeley Heights, NJ 07922 | Hants GU12 6BP |
| USA | UK |

http://www.enslow.com

**Library of Congress Cataloging-in-Publication Data**

Aretha, David.
 The Detroit Pistons basketball team / David Aretha.
  p. cm. — (Great sports teams)
 Includes bibliographical references and index.
 ISBN 0-7660-1487-8
  1. Detroit Pistons (Basketball team)—History—Juvenile literature.
 [1. Detroit Pistons (Basketball team)—History. 2. Basketball—History.] I. Title.
 II. Series.
 GV885.52.D47 A74    2001
 796.323′64′0977434—dc21

                                                    00-012217

Printed in the United States of America

10 9 8 7 6 5 4 3 2 1

**To Our Readers:** We have done our best to make sure all Internet addresses in this book were active and appropriate when we went to press. However, the author and the publisher have no control over and assume no liability for the material available on those Internet sites or on other Web sites they may link to. Any comments or suggestions can be sent by e-mail to comments@enslow.com or to the address on the back cover.

**Illustration Credits:** AP/Wide World Photos.

**Cover Illustration:** AP/Wide World Photos.

**Cover Description:** Jerry Stackhouse.

# CONTENTS

*The Lakers' Magic Johnson defends against his good friend and fellow point guard Isiah Thomas during the second half of game six of the 1988 NBA Finals.*

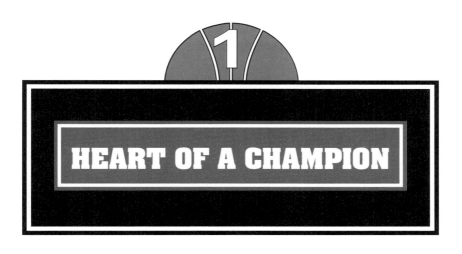

# HEART OF A CHAMPION

siah Thomas had waited his entire NBA career for this moment. Yet there he was—trying to bear the pain of an injured ankle that would eventually swell to the size of a melon.

The end of the 1987–88 season was the first appearance in the NBA Finals for the star point guard and his Detroit Pistons teammates. Their opponents, the Los Angeles Lakers, were trying to win their second straight championship. A friendly rivalry was at stake, too. Thomas and star Lakers guard Magic Johnson had become close friends over the years, and Isiah wanted dearly to earn a championship ring for bragging rights.

Yet in the third quarter of game six at the L.A. Forum, after Thomas had hit the Lakers for 14 second-half points to spark a Detroit rally, it happened. Thomas landed on Laker guard Michael Cooper's foot after passing to Joe Dumars on a fast break. Thomas winced in pain.

"I can't believe this is happening," Thomas thought as he lay looking up at the Forum rafters where the Lakers had hung numerous banners. "Not now. Not fifteen minutes away from an NBA championship."[1]

## A Slow Climb

It had been a slow climb to the to the NBA Finals for Thomas and the Pistons. By 1988, Detroit had been a playoff team for five straight seasons. Three years before, they finished second in the division and made it to the second round of the playoffs. The team then took a step backward in 1985–86, finishing third in the division and getting eliminated in the first round. Then, in the 1986–87 season, they finished second in the Central Division and made it all the way to the Conference Finals before being eliminated by the then-defending NBA champs, the Boston Celtics.

Now, a year later, the Pistons were closer to a championship than ever before. As Thomas sat on the bench receiving treatment for his ankle, he recalled a time a few years earlier when he and Mark Aguirre were watching a basketball game on television. It was an important game, and in it, a player had sat out while a separated shoulder healed. Thomas and Aguirre agreed that if ever a similar situation arose for either of them, they would play no matter what.

"I told him I'd have to be dead for them to keep me out of the lineup," Thomas recalled.[2]

***D***etroit Pistons Dennis Rodman and Joe Dumars defend the inbound pass of the Lakers' James Worthy during game six of the 1988 NBA Finals.

So on June 19, 1988, Thomas stayed true to his word and did the only thing he could think of at the time. He pushed the pain aside and put on his brightest boyish smile. He then convinced team trainer Mike Abdenour to talk with Head Coach Chuck Daly. "Tell Chuck I'm ready to go back in," Thomas said.[3]

### "Out of This World"

Back in Thomas went, and he didn't miss a beat. Over one stretch, he scored 14 straight Pistons points. In that span, he nailed two free throws, four jumpers, a bank shot, and a layup. He finished the third quarter with 25 points, a Finals record for the most in one period. *Los Angeles Times* sports columnist Mike Downey wrote: "He was out of this world. . . He was making shots off the wrong foot, off the glass, off the wall."[4]

Thomas put the Pistons ahead by an 81–79 score, and they clung to a 102–99 edge with one minute to play. Byron Scott made a big jumper for the Lakers. The great Kareem Abdul-Jabbar added two free throws, forcing the Pistons to play from behind in the final seconds. A collision between Thomas and teammate Adrian Dantley foiled Detroit's chance for a final shot, with the Lakers claiming a 103–102 victory. Isiah's 43 points were two too few.

After the game, Thomas said his ankle was the size of a basketball. A stretch? Perhaps a bit. However, those who witnessed his heroics felt that the size of Isiah's heart was ten times greater than the size of his swollen ankle.

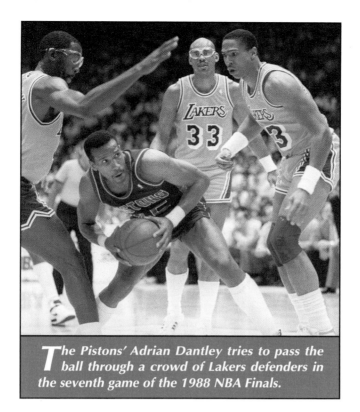

*The Pistons' Adrian Dantley tries to pass the ball through a crowd of Lakers defenders in the seventh game of the 1988 NBA Finals.*

The Lakers' win tied the series at three games apiece. Over the next two days, Thomas spent most of his time in the training facility of the Los Angeles Raiders football team, trying to get ready for game seven. The swelling subsided, but Thomas could barely walk. He started the last game but was unable to save the Pistons from a 108–105 loss, as the Lakers repeated as champs.

The series was hardly a waste for Thomas and the Pistons, though. They learned what it took to reach the top, lessons that would help them win titles of their own over the next two years. And they sent a strong message to their toughest NBA rivals: As long as Detroit and its star guard could stand upright, the Pistons would be a force.

*G*eorge Yardley (12) of the Fort Wayne Pistons battles against Ernie Beck (7) of the Philadelphia Warriors in game three of the 1956 NBA Finals.

# PISTONS HISTORY

One would think that with the name Pistons, the team originated in the Motor City—the nickname for Detroit. Not true. The club was actually born in 1937, in Fort Wayne, Indiana, when Fred Zollner assembled a team for an industrial league. Zollner owned a factory that made pistons for automobiles, so the name was a natural choice.

## The Early Years

The Fort Wayne Pistons joined the National Basketball League (NBL) in 1941, winning the NBL title in 1944 and again in 1945. In 1949, the NBL merged with the Basketball Association of America (BAA) to form the NBA. The club then went through a few disappointing seasons before regaining success. With former referee Charlie Eckman as head coach, Fort Wayne beat Minneapolis to reach the 1955 NBA Finals. There,

Eckmann's quintet lost a seven-game war to the Syracuse Nationals.

The Pistons made it back-to-back Western Division titles the next year, but the Philadelphia Warriors beat them out for the title. Soon, Zollner decided to move the team to a larger market to keep up with a growing league. And what better place for the Pistons than the automobile capital of the world, Detroit, Michigan?

## Detroit's New Team

Detroit loved its new team, even though it struggled on the court. Perhaps the most memorable Pistons highlight from those early days came in 1957–58. That year, George Yardley's final bucket made him the first NBA player to score 2,000 points (actually 2,001) in a season.

In 1967–68, All-Star guard Dave Bing swished 27.1 points per game—tops in the league. In the early 1970s, big-footed center Bob Lanier pushed the Pistons to some of their best seasons.

It wasn't until the 1980s, however, that the Pistons hit on all cylinders. The club grew into a championship operation and even a league trend-setter. With such stars as Isiah Thomas, Bill Laimbeer, Joe Dumars, Mark Aguirre, and Adrian Dantley, the Pistons joined the NBA elite.

Longtime play-by-play man George Blaha blared such phrases as "eyes it, flies it" and "guns it, gets it." Fans flocked in record numbers to see sixth man Vinnie "the Microwave" Johnson, who heated up fast. Blaha went wild over a young Dennis Rodman. Before

*The Pistons' Dave Bing looks to pass the ball against the Lakers in 1967.*

indulging in tattoos, rings, and controversy in later years, The Worm dominated the boards and smothered opponents with his defense.

And if winning wasn't enough to keep fans entertained, the Pistons also had John Salley. An amateur comedian in his spare time, Spider was the quick-witted pitch man who never met a stage he didn't like. "I'm not a jock," he once said. "I'm an entertainer."[1]

The Pistons drew enormous crowds to the cavernous Silverdome, including an NBA-record 61,983 on January 29, 1988. That fall, the team unveiled a more basketball-friendly arena: the sparkling Palace of

*R*ick Mahorn rips the ball from the grasp of the Chicago Bulls' Scottie Pippen. Mahorn's rough playing style helped earn the Detroit Pistons the nickname "Bad Boys."

Auburn Hills. Now that the team had one of the finest homes in pro basketball, one of its next moves was to improve its time on the road. Why fight those delays and crowds on commercial airplanes when you can relax in your own jet?

## *Travelling In Style*

It was an idea offered by pilot Chuck Shipp, and it sounded like a great one to the Pistons. Owner Bill Davidson turned an eighty-four-seat jet into a luxurious, twenty-four-seat model with two televisions, two VCRs, and a stereo.[2] The cost was more than the team would have paid to fly commercially. However, the team's first two seasons in the plane ended with a trip to the Finals in 1988 and the team's first NBA championship in 1989. Who could argue with that?

The Pistons added another title in 1990 and were the envy of the league in many respects. They were also hated, by many, for a bruising style of play that earned them the nickname "Bad Boys." Laimbeer and the powerful Rick Mahorn were never afraid to play physical and mix things up.

But by 1991, the Pistons were forced to make way for Michael Jordan and the rival Chicago Bulls. That year, the Bulls finally defeated the Pistons after several close playoff series in earlier years. In 1994, the Pistons began to rebuild their team around explosive forward Grant Hill. Hill was a classy gentleman, the antithesis of the Bad Boy image.

*B*ob Lanier (16) of the Pistons tries to block the shot of the Bulls' Artis Gilmore (53) during a game in 1976.

# THE STARS

**E**ven in their sub-.500 seasons, the Pistons often featured a special player who gave fans their money's worth. Several such standouts teamed up in the Motor City in the 1980s, when winning became the Pistons way. Featured here are the five best players in franchise history.

## Dave Bing

Dave Bing's court vision was truly phenomenal—especially considering the damage to his eyes. When he was five, his left eye was accidentally poked with a nail. An operation saved him from blindness, but his left-side vision was never fully clear.

A star at Syracuse University, Bing was chosen second overall in the 1966 NBA draft by Detroit. He averaged 20 points per game that season (his career average) as a star in the making. However, in 1970, he suffered a partially detached retina in his right eye.

With blurred vision, he worked to become a better defensive player in case he couldn't score enough.

Bing's best asset, though, was his passing. He could penetrate into the teeth of any defense and set up teammates for open shots. As a player, Bing was known for his tremendous determination and heart. Today he is one of Detroit's most successful and charitable businessmen.

### Bob Lanier

Bob Lanier owned "the two biggest feets in basketball," according to a popular television commercial. He wore size twenty-two sneakers, which in fact preceded him (in bronze) into the Hall of Fame.[1] His feats were special, too.

A hulking center from St. Bonaventure University, Lanier burst onto the NBA scene in 1970. The six-foot-eleven, 265-pound Lanier displayed a feathery shooting touch rare for a man his size. The Dobber, a left-hander, scored 40 or more points 20 times in his career. He was also a monster shot-blocker.

Only two players earned more NBA MVP votes in 1974, after Lanier averaged 22.5 points and 13.3 rebounds per game. He was traded in 1980 to the Milwaukee Bucks and won five division titles there. Unfortunately, his king-sized shoes never stepped into an NBA Finals game.

### Isiah Thomas

He flashed his innocent smile to soften officials, then spoke bashfully to the media afterward. In such situations, Isiah Thomas was genuine. Yet beneath his

*The Detroit Pistons Basketball Team*

boyish grin was a fiercely determined All-Star with a killer instinct on the court.

Though a smallish six foot one, Thomas could penetrate and score at will. After leading Indiana to the national championship in 1981, he was welcomed as a savior in Detroit. In 1984–85, Zeke set an NBA record with 1,123 assists. In both 1984 and 1986, he earned the NBA All-Star game MVP award.

*Isiah Thomas is widely considered one of the best point guards ever. He led the Pistons to back-to-back titles in 1989 and 1990.*

With Thomas running the offense, the Pistons made the NBA Finals in 1988 and won championships in 1989 and 1990. He is considered by many to be one of the best pure point guards ever to have played the game.

In 2000, Thomas was elected to the Basketball Hall of Fame. That same year, he also took over as head coach of the Indiana Pacers.

### Joe Dumars

Michael Jordan said that no one guarded him better than Joe Dumars. As his career wore on, Joe D also gained respect as a complete off-guard and the ultimate professional.

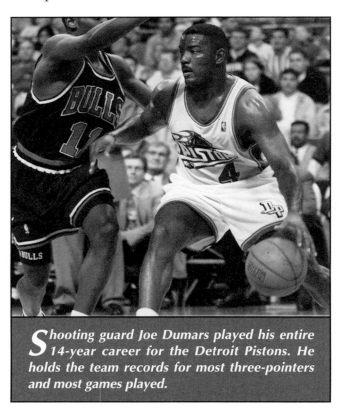

*Shooting guard Joe Dumars played his entire 14-year career for the Detroit Pistons. He holds the team records for most three-pointers and most games played.*

*The Detroit Pistons Basketball Team*

A McNeese State grad, Dumars joined his idol, Isiah Thomas, in the Pistons backcourt in 1985. If some thought Dumars was only tough on defense, he proved them wrong in a 1989 Finals sweep of the L.A. Lakers. He averaged 27.3 points a game in the series and was named Finals MVP.

The following year, Dumars averaged 18.2 points in 20 playoff games as Detroit won again. By the time Joe wrapped up his fourteen-year career in 1999, he had played more games (1,018) and canned more three-pointers (990) than anyone in team history. He went on to become the club's General Manager.

---

## Grant Hill

On the court, Grant Hill explodes to the hoop for nasty dunks. In the locker room, he impresses the press with his grace and intelligence. In fact, he has been named to the All-NBA first team and the league's All-Interview first team.

In 1999–2000, Hill averaged 25.8 points per game. A six-foot eight-inch point forward, he is also one of the league's most versatile players. In three different seasons, he paced Detroit in scoring, rebounding, and assists.

"We have the best player in the NBA—the best non-center in the NBA for sure," said Pistons coach Alvin Gentry in January 2000. "I believe that, and I will go to my grave believing that."[2]

Unfortunately for Pistons fans, Hill left the team at the end of the season as a free agent, signing with the Orlando Magic.

*D*ave DeBusschere speaks to a press gathering on February 13, 2000. DeBusschere served as both a player and coach to the Pistons.

# THE LEADERS

From twenty-four-year-old player/coach Dave DeBusschere to NBA Coach of the Year Ray Scott, the Pistons have employed legendary leaders. None was more colorful than Dick Vitale; none more successful than Chuck Daly. Here's a look at the men in charge.

## *Dave DeBusschere*

Recently, Dave DeBusschere was asked if he'd like to coach in the NBA. He said no. "I think it would be an overwhelming job," he added, "and I don't think my personality is geared for coaching."[1]

The Pistons thought DeBusschere was just the man when, in 1964, they made the Detroit native their player/coach at age twenty-four. DeBusschere became the youngest coach in the history of the NBA. Unfortunately, Double D was better at sticking to his defenders like glue than at drawing Xs and Os. He was traded to the Knicks when his contract expired in 1967.

DeBusschere helped New York to NBA championships in 1970 and 1973. He played in eight All-Star games and was voted by the NBA as one of the fifty greatest players of all time.

### Ray Scott

Eleven different men coached the Pistons in their first sixteen seasons of pro basketball. The eleventh was something special. Ray Scott was a former Pistons player whose line-drive shot helped him score more than 10,000 career points. Through the 2000–01 season, he remained the only Detroit boss to be honored as NBA Coach of the Year.

Scott took the Pistons' coaching reins at age thirty-four in 1972–73. His goal was to steer the team in a winning direction for the first time since its move from Fort Wayne in 1957. He did it in a unique way. Some called him "mystical." He called himself the "Cheese," quoting the old nursery rhyme "The Farmer in the Dell," which says "the cheese stands alone."[2]

Scott stood alone among NBA coaches in 1973–74. Detroit won a team-record 52 games and made the playoffs for the first time in seven years.

### Dick Vitale

Love him or hate him, every college basketball fan knows him. "It's awesome, bay-beeeeee," shouts Dick Vitale each game night on ESPN.

*The Detroit Pistons Basketball Team*

*B*efore gaining fame as a sports analyst for ESPN, Dick Vitale served as Head Coach of the Pistons for the 1978–1979 season.

Back in the 1970s, Dickie V rah-rahed the University of Detroit into an NCAA tournament team. He became a local hero, and the Pistons decided to tap into his enthusiasm. Unfortunately, the team went 30–52 in his one full season as head coach in 1978–79.

At the press conference for the 1979 NBA draft, Vitale brought boxes of Special K to celebrate the drafting of Greg Kelser. However, Detroit got off to a soggy start (4–8) and Vitale was let go. "I think he was cut out to be a great college coach," said Richie Adubato, Vitale's assistant with the Pistons.[3]

### Jack McCloskey

His nickname was Trader Jack, and everyone knew it. More than once, McCloskey sent faxes to every team in the NBA, telling them that every player on his team was available for a trade.[4]

As Pistons general manager, McCloskey played the NBA version of *Let's Make a Deal*. His first trade sent star center Bob Lanier to Milwaukee for Kent Benson and a first-round draft choice. His moves in the 1980s helped the Pistons build a championship club.

McCloskey's draft picks included Isiah Thomas, Kelly Tripucka, and Joe Dumars. Even when the Pistons were winning, Jack rolled the dice. He traded one of the team's most popular players, Adrian Dantley, for Mark Aguirre in 1988. Months later, Detroit won the first of its back-to-back championships.

### Chuck Daly

Like a child hoping his 25-cent shopping-mall ride lasts longer than a few minutes, Chuck Daly arrived in Detroit hoping to stay for a while. "To be honest," he said, "I didn't know if I would last one season. They'd had something like ten coaches in eleven years. I looked at Scotty [Robertson] before me, and I said to myself, 'I don't know if I can do a better job than this guy.'"[5]

Daly lasted nine seasons, and now it's other Detroit coaches who struggle to match his success.

**H**ead Coach Chuck Daly led the Pistons to two consecutive championships. His "Jordan Rules" was one of the few defensive schemes to slow down Michael Jordan.

He was known for his dapper suits, great hair, and dedication to defense. His Jordan Rules made up the only defensive scheme ever to slow down Michael Jordan.

Daly's work in Detroit was remarkable. Try blending the personalities of Dennis Rodman, Bill Laimbeer, Isiah Thomas, Rick Mahorn, and others into a championship team. Daly succeeded in doing so twice.

**D**ennis Rodman was moved into the starting line-up prior to the 1986–87 season. His presence helped make the Pistons a much more defensive-minded team.

# GLORY DAYS

siah Thomas certainly remembers some of the greatest Pistons teams of all time. Thomas sped the Pistons to 186 points in a 1983 game, then led the defensive-minded Bad Boys to two—and almost three—NBA titles.

### 1983-84

Detroit at Denver, December 13, 1983. Once the ball was tossed up at midcourt, the Pistons and Nuggets treated 9,655 fans to the highest scoring game in NBA history. It took three overtimes to decide, with Detroit outlasting Denver, 186–184.

Former Piston Bill Laimbeer keeps the box score hanging on his office wall to this day. "My attorney was in his car in Chicago listening to the game," he said. "But it was a faint signal . . . so he kept driving around the city trying to get it to come in better. He spent three hours driving around, waiting for the game to end."[1]

When it did, finally, the Nuggets' Kiki Vandeweghe had 51 points, and Detroit's Isiah Thomas had 47. John Long's dunk in the third OT put the Pistons on top for keeps. The teams broke six NBA records that night, including most players with 40-plus points (four).

The Pistons finished the season at 49–33. They lost the opening playoff series to New York, dropping the decisive game five in overtime.

---

## 1986-88

Coach Chuck Daly did not get down on his Pistons after Atlanta eliminated them in the first round of the 1986 playoffs. Instead, he stood in front of the team and guaranteed them that they were going to win a championship.

Six months later, the quest began. Dennis Rodman was moved into the starting five for rebounding and defense. The Pistons traded Kent Benson and Kelly Tripucka to Utah for two-time scoring champion Adrian Dantley. Detroit won 52 games in 1986–87, took two playoff series, and pushed Boston to seven games in the Eastern Conference Finals.

The next season produced a 54–28 record and the Pistons' first Central Division crown. A seven-game loss to the Los Angeles Lakers in the 1988 Finals was a heartbreaker, but the team was poised for a championship breakthrough. "We wished the new season could start the next day," said Isiah Thomas.[2]

*The Detroit Pistons Basketball Team*

*John Salley tries to avoid Michael Jordan during game four of the 1990 NBA Eastern Conference Finals. The Bulls pushed the Pistons to seven games before being eliminated that year.*

## 1988–89

Isiah Thomas had never been happier to greet an old friend. His boyhood pal from Chicago, Mark Aguirre, arrived in Detroit in a trade for Adrian Dantley during the 1988–89 season. Fans expected him to be the last piece of a championship puzzle.

The Pistons' rugged style had earned them the nickname "Bad Boys." Their 63–19 record in 1988–89 was the best in the NBA and tops in team history. They took six games to eliminate the Bulls in the Eastern

Finals, but they swept past their other three playoff opponents. That included the defending champion Lakers in the Finals.

Detroit's guards smoked L.A. in game one of the Finals, and a Pistons comeback led to victory in game two. When the Lakers' Magic Johnson was injured in a fall in game three, Detroit motored to the title. Pistons

**B**ill Laimbeer watches as Isiah Thomas shoots around the Portland Trailblazers' Jerome Kersey in game one of the 1990 NBA Finals.

*The Detroit Pistons Basketball Team*

guard Joe Dumars, with 27.3 PPG, was named NBA Finals MVP.

## 1989-90

Detroit repeated as Central Division champion in 1989–90 (59–23), but not without a fight from Michael Jordan's Chicago Bulls. Jordan haunted the Pistons all through the Eastern Conference Finals. In the end, Detroit's defense was too much in a 93–74 game seven victory.

Next up were the Portland Trail Blazers. Although the Pistons won in five games, each game was a war. In the opener, Portland led by ten points before a ferocious shooting spree by Isiah Thomas pushed Detroit to victory. The Blazers came back to win the second game in overtime. After game two, Joe Dumars was told that his father had died. On the very next outing, the All-Star guard erupted for 26 points.

Detroit took game four, 112–109. Vinnie Johnson sank the winning shot late in the fifth and final game, and the Pistons were on top of the world again.

*T*he Pistons' Grant Hill slam dunks over George Lynch of the Philadelphia 76ers in a game from December 1999.

# HORSEPOWER

ome may wonder why the Pistons' team logo features a stallion. The answer is in one word: horsepower.

The 1999–2000 Pistons took fans on a thrill ride with their turbo-charged offense. Led by superstar Grant Hill and hard-driving Jerry Stackhouse, the Pistons rocked the house with clever passes, slam dunks, and long-range bombs.

Detroit was the No. 2 scoring team in the NBA. It was the first time in the fifty-two years of the franchise that they ranked so high in offense. Only Sacramento put the ball in the net at a faster pace than the Pistons, who averaged 104 points per game.

## A Growing Team

From 1994 to 1999, the Pistons posted a winning record and reached the NBA playoffs four out of five seasons. This success only made the team and its loyal fans hungry for more. In fact, the Pistons replaced Head Coach Alvin Gentry in 1999–2000 in an effort to climb in the league standings.

Under Gentry and new coach George Irvine, Detroit earned its second straight winning record (42-40), good for seventh place in the Eastern Conference. "We won more games than I thought we would," Irvine said.[1]

Hill and Stackhouse formed one of the best one-two punches in basketball, pouring in a combined 49.4 points per game. Among teammates, only Los Angeles Lakers Shaquille O'Neal and Kobe Bryant scored more. Hill, who ran the Pistons as their point forward, ranked third in the NBA in scoring at 25.8 points per game.

Stackhouse, a master at driving to the hoop and drawing the foul, poured in 23.6 points per game. Like Hill, he represented Detroit at the NBA All-Star Game. Lindsay Hunter, Christian Laettner, and Terry Mills rounded out the Pistons' regular starting five. Hunter ranked third in the NBA in swished three-pointers with 168. Reserve forward Jerome Williams finished ninth in the league in rebounding at 9.6 per night. He also shot a sterling .564 from the floor.

### The New Millennium

Hill opened the new millennium as basketball's hottest player. He scorched Orlando and Atlanta for 42 points each on January 3 and 5. Though fatigued the next day, he willed in 19 fourth-quarter points to down Milwaukee. "When we needed him to step up,

*The Detroit Pistons Basketball Team*

*J*erry Stackhouse is congratulated by teammate Joe Smith after scoring in a game against the Boston Celtics on December 26, 2000.

he stepped up big," said Gentry.[2] It gave Detroit six straight triumphs—their longest winning streak since 1992. "We know if we play the right way, we can beat anyone in the East," reserve Michael Curry said.[3]

Unfortunately, the Pistons have not played their best ball in recent playoff trips. They have not advanced past the first round since 1991. In 2000, Hill broke his left ankle during the team's first-round playoff loss to Miami. Then, after the season, he left the Pistons to sign with the Orlando Magic as a free agent.

Stackhouse, never one to hold back his feelings, said the team needs to upgrade at the point guard, power forward, and center positions. He said he did not mean to anger any of his current teammates. He simply wants to win.

*Isiah Thomas shakes hands with Joe Dumars on "Joe Dumars Night" at the Palace of Auburn Hills, March 10, 2000.*

*The Detroit Pistons Basketball Team*

### Remembering the Past

Win or lose, the Pistons treat their fans right. Their home, the Palace of Auburn Hills, has been voted Arena of the Year by *Performance* magazine seven times. The sound system is out of this world. When the Pistons are winning and the music's blaring, their house really rocks.

Such was the case on March 10, 2000—Joe Dumars Night at the Palace. The Pistons honored Joe D, the classiest and perhaps most beloved player in club history. They raised his No. 4 jersey to the rafters, where it joined those of Bad Boys Isiah Thomas, Vinnie Johnson, and Bill Laimbeer. As Detroit native Aretha Franklin sang the national anthem, fans reminisced about the team's championship years. It was a great night to be a Pistons fan.

# STATISTICS

## Team Record

### The Pistons History

| YEARS | LOCATION | W | L | PCT. | CHAMPIONSHIPS |
|---|---|---|---|---|---|
| 1948–49 to 1956–57 | Fort Wayne | 313 | 306 | .506 | Western Division, 1955–56 |
| 1957–58 to 1959–60 | Detroit | 91 | 128 | .416 | None |
| 1960–61 to 1969–70 | Detroit | 314 | 492 | .390 | None |
| 1970–71 to 1979–80 | Detroit | 367 | 453 | .448 | None |
| 1980–81 to 1989–90 | Detroit | 466 | 354 | .568 | Central Division, 1988–90<br>Eastern Conference, 1988–<br>NBA Champs, 1989–90 |
| 1990–91 to 1999–2000 | Detroit | 394 | 394 | .500 | None |

### The Pistons Today

| SEASON | SEASON RECORD | PLAYOFF RECORD | HEAD COACH | DIVISION FINIS |
|---|---|---|---|---|
| 1990–91 | 50–32 | 7–8 | Chuck Daly | 2nd |
| 1991–92 | 48–34 | 2–3 | Chuck Daly | 3rd |
| 1992–93 | 40–42 | 0–0 | Ron Rothstein | 6th |
| 1993–94 | 20–62 | 0–0 | Don Chaney | 6th |
| 1994–95 | 28–54 | 0–0 | Don Chaney | 7th |
| 1995–96 | 46–36 | 0–3 | Doug Collins | 4th (tie) |
| 1996–97 | 54–28 | 2–3 | Doug Collins | 3rd (tie) |
| 1997–98 | 37–45 | 0–0 | Doug Collins/<br>Alvin Gentry | 6th |
| 1998–99 | 29–21 | 2–3 | Alvin Gentry | 3rd |
| 1999–2000 | 42–40 | 0–3 | Alvin Gentry/<br>George Irvine | 4th |

*The Detroit Pistons Basketball Team*

## Total History

| SEASON RECORD | PLAYOFF RECORD | NBA CHAMPIONSHIPS |
|---|---|---|
| 1,945–2,127 | 116–117 | 2 |

## Coaching Records

| COACH | YEARS COACHED | RECORD | CHAMPIONSHIPS |
|---|---|---|---|
| Carl Bennett | 1948 | 0–6 | None |
| Paul Armstrong | 1948–49 | 22-32 | None |
| Murray Mendenhall | 1949–51 | 72–64 | None |
| Paul Birch | 1951–54 | 105–102 | None |
| Charles Eckman | 1954–57 | 123–118 | Western Division, 1955–56 |
| Red Rocha | 1958–59 | 65–88 | None |
| Dick McGuire | 1959–63 | 122–158 | None |
| Charles Wolf | 1963–64 | 25–66 | None |
| Dave DeBusschere | 1964–67 | 79–143 | None |
| Donnis Butcher | 1967–68 | 52–60 | None |
| Paul Seymour | 1969–70 | 22–38 | None |
| Bill van Breda Kolff | 1970–71 | 82–92 | None |
| Terry Dischinger | 1971–72 | 0–2 | None |
| Earl Lloyd | 1972–73 | 22–55 | None |
| Ray Scott | 1973–75 | 147–134 | None |
| Herb Brown | 1976–77 | 72–74 | None |
| Bob Kauffman | 1977–78 | 29–29 | None |
| Dick Vitale | 1978–79 | 34–60 | None |
| Richie Adubato | 1979–80 | 12–58 | None |
| Scotty Robertson | 1980–83 | 97–149 | None |

# Coaching Records (continued)

| COACH | YEARS COACHED | RECORD | CHAMPIONSHIPS |
|---|---|---|---|
| Chuck Daly | 1983–92 | 467–271 | NBA Champions, 1989, 1990<br>Eastern Conference, 1988–90<br>Central Division, 1988–9( |
| Ron Rothstein | 1992–93 | 40–42 | None |
| Don Chaney | 1993–95 | 48–116 | None |
| Doug Collins | 1995–97 | 121–88 | None |
| Alvin Gentry | 1997–99 | 73–71 | None |
| George Irvine | 1999–2000 | 14–10 | None |

## Ten Great Pistons

| PLAYER | SEA | YRS | G | REB | AST | STL | BLK | PTS | A |
|---|---|---|---|---|---|---|---|---|---|
| George Yardley | 1953–59 | 7 | 384 | 3,537 | 668 | * | *| | 7,339 | 1 |
| Dave Bing | 1966–75 | 12 | 675 | 2,828 | 4,330 | 225* | 43* | 15,235 | 2 |
| Bob Lanier | 1970–80 | 14 | 681 | 8,063 | 2,256 | 466* | 799* | 15,488 | 2 |
| Isiah Thomas | 1981–94 | 13 | 979 | 3,478 | 9,061 | 1,861 | 249 | 18,882 | 1 |
| Joe Dumars | 1985–99 | 14 | 1,018 | 2,203 | 4,612 | 902 | 83 | 16,401 | 1 |
| Kelly Tripucka | 1981–86 | 10 | 352 | 1,582 | 1,405 | 363 | 77 | 7,597 | 2 |
| Vinnie Johnson | 1981–91 | 13 | 798 | 2,491 | 2,661 | 714 | 215 | 10,146 | 1 |
| Bill Laimbeer | 1982–94 | 14 | 937 | 9,430 | 1,923 | 654 | 887 | 11,527 | 1 |
| Dennis Rodman | 1986–93 | 14 | 549 | 6,299 | 715 | 401 | 399 | 4,844 | 8 |
| Grant Hill | 1994–2000 | 6 | 435 | 3,416 | 2,720 | 694 | 281 | 9,390 | 2 |

*Statistics are incomplete for some players in some categories. The NBA did not keep statistics for steals and blocks until the 1973–74 season.

SEA=Seasons with Pistons   REB=Rebounds   BLK=Blocks
YRS=Years in NBA   AST=Assists   PTS=Points
G=Games   STL=Steals   AVG=Scoring average

*The Detroit Pistons Basketball Team*

# CHAPTER NOTES

### Chapter 1. Heart of a Champion

1. Isiah Thomas with Matt Dobek, *Bad Boys! An Inside Look at the Detroit Pistons' 1988–89 Championship Season*, (Grand Rapids, Mich.: Masters Press, 1989), p. 51.

2. Ibid., p. 51.

3. Ibid.

4. Mike Downey, "Thomas Is Bloody, Not Yet Beaten," *Los Angeles Times*, June 20, 1988, Section 3, p. 1.

### Chapter 2. Pistons History

1. Rick Ratliff, "John Salley," *Bad Boys* (Detroit Free Press compilation, 1989), p. 45.

2. Drew Sharp, "The Plane," *Bad Boys* (Detroit Free Press compilation, 1989), p. 49.

### Chapter 3. The Stars

1. Nick Russo, *Basketball Legends* (Lincolnwood, Ill.: Publications International, Ltd., 1996), p. 114.

2. Chris McCosky, "Hill Leads Pistons' Rally," *The Detroit News*, January 6, 2000, Sports, p. 1.

### Chapter 4. The Leaders

1. "NBA Legends Dave DeBusschere," NBA History, n.d., <http://www.nba.com/history/debusschere_bio.html> (November 30, 2000).

2. Jerry Green, "Whatever Happened to Ray Scott?" *The Detroit News*, March 9, 1997, Sports, p 5.

3. Mike Celizic, "Vitale's Life Is Awesome, Bay-Bee," *The Bergen Record* (New Jersey), March 31, 1996, Sports, p. 1.

4. Charlie Vincent, "Jack McCloskey," *Bad Boys* (Detroit Free Press compilation, 1989), p. 54.

5. Mitch Albom, "Chuck Daly," *Bad Boys* (Detroit Free Press compilation, 1989), pp. 17–18.

### Chapter 5. Glory Days

1. Charlie Vincent, "Nothing But Net," *Hoop*, March 2000, p. 63.

2. Isiah Thomas with Matt Dobek, *Bad Boys! An Inside Look at the Detroit Pistons' 1988–89 Championship Season* (Grand Rapids, Mich.: Masters Press, 1989), p. 53.

### Chapter 6. Horsepower

1. "Pistons Team Report," *SportsLine.com Reports*, June, 2000, <http://www.sportsline.com/u/basketball/nba/teams/insider/pistons.htm> (November 30, 2000).

2. Chris McCosky, "Hill leads Pistons' rally," *The Detroit News*, January 6, 2000, Sports, p. 1.

3. "Pistons Team Report," *SportsLine.com Reports*, January, 2000, <http://www.sportsline.com/u/basketball/nba/teams/insider/pistons.htm> (November 30, 2000).

# GLOSSARY

**alley-oop pass**—A lob pass in which the receiving player leaps, catches the ball, and dunks it in one fluid motion.

**assist**—A pass to a player who shoots and scores.

**Bad Boys**—Nickname for the Detroit Pistons from the late 1980s, based on the team's hard-nosed, physical, defensive style of play.

**center**—Usually the biggest player on the team. Plays close to the basket and requires strong rebounding and inside scoring skills.

**fast break**—Through passing and dribbling, the offensive team races the ball down court toward the basket.

**field goal**—Any shot attempted during the course of play, excluding free throws. It's always worth two points unless it's attempted from behind the three-point line.

**free throw**—An uncontested shot from a line 15 feet from the basket. Such shots are awarded when a player is fouled in the act of attempting a field goal.

**jumper**—A shot attempted, from at least a few feet from the basket, after a player leaps into the air. Also called a jump shot.

**NBA draft**—Annual process in which each NBA team selects the best eligible players, usually from college.

**NBA Finals**—The league's best-of-seven championship series featuring the Eastern Conference champion vs. the Western Conference champion.

**overtime**—An extra five-minute period that occurs when the score is tied after the regulation four quarters.

**point guard**—The player usually responsible for dribbling the ball up the court and starting the offense with a pass.

**point forward**—A small forward who is such a skilled ball-handler that he often leads the offensive attack.

**rebound**—The retrieval of a missed shot.

**three-point shot**—A field goal that's worth three points. The shot is taken from behind a line that ranges from 22 feet to 23 feet, nine inches from the rim.

# FURTHER READING

Addy, Steve. *The Detroit Pistons: Four Decades of Motor City Memories*. Champaign, Ill.: Sagamore Publishing, Inc., 1997.

Italia, Bob. *Detroit Pistons*. Edina, Minn.: Abdo & Daughters, 1997.

Knapp, Ron. *Sports Great Isiah Thomas*. Berkeley Heights, N.J.: Enslow Publishers, 1992.

Rambeck, Richard. *Detroit Pistons*. Mankato, Minn.: Creative Education, Inc., 1997.

Sachare, Alex, ed. *The NBA's Official Encyclopedia of Pro Basketball*. New York: Villard Books, 1994.

Schleichert, Elizabeth. *Dave Bing: Basketball Great with a Heart*. Berkeley Heights, N.J.: Enslow Publishers, 1995.

Thornley, Stew. *Sports Great Dennis Rodman*. Berkeley Heights, N.J.: Enslow Publishers, 1996.

Vancil, Mark, ed. *NBA at 50*. New York: Park Lane Press, 1996.

# INDEX

## WHERE TO WRITE AND INTERNET SITES

http://www.nba.com/

http://sports.espn.go.com/
nba/index

http://sportsillustrated.cnn.com/
basketball/nba/teams/pistons/

http://pistons.rivals.com/default.
asp?sid=613

The Detroit Pistons
The Palace of Auburn Hills
Two Championship Drive
Auburn Hills, MI 48326